Hurricane Dreams

Gerald Braude

Contents

Conversations with the Wind

I want to be a tribal member.
Why on earth would you want to do that?
So I can dig for razor clams on the beach.
Sorry but you'll have to do better than that.
So I can get discounts at the pump.
Sorry but you can do better than that.
So I can be a card carrying member, like American Express.
Sorry but that's insane.
So I can ... because the reservation is dry.
(the throats clear)
I understand but do you have any bloodlines?
Not that I'm aware of.
Then we can't help you.
Okay then I want to convert to Judaism.
Why in God's name would you want to do that?
Again, so I can have a card, the one with the Jewish le'om on it.
That privilege requires arduous ritual pools approved by the
courts.
On second thought, I'll convert to Islam.
Why in Allah's name would you want to do that?
Because the Qur'an forbids alcohol.
Good point, but you have traces of Jewish blood, correct?
Half, actually.
Sorry, no dice.
How come?
Because, as far as we're concerned, it's never been done before.
In that case, I'd rather be a Catholic.
You better be or else we'll burn you at the stake.

The Fine Art of Editing a Flashback

I just turned twenty-one and still have zits.

The black literature professor swaggers into the classroom
with a sting of Brute aftershave. Muscles bulge from
his three-piece suit. He wears round, wired-rimmed glasses.

He bellows, "I'm going to be tough." Our hair blows back.
We sink into our seats and return a near-frozen nod.

I just turned sixty-one, and scars have replaced my zits.

The same professor swaggers into the classroom with his
Brute, muscles, three-piece suit, and glasses.

He bellows, "I'm going to be tough." I relax back into my chair
and say, "Will you cut the bullshit and just get to the material."

Reflections from a High Plains Farmer

Whenever I till my chemical-free soil,
and let me my mind drift elsewhere,
I often wonder, as I do now,
So, who is this guy?

Yes, he has the big CEO title.
Yes, he has a cozy rapport with the government.
At least, better than the one I have.
And yes, he's much better groomed than I.

But does he have more than a blank face?
Is he married, or better yet still married.
Does he rear more than just factory-farmed chicks?
And of those that he does rear, are they human?

And if so, I'll bet you my acreage that they attend
the best schools money can buy.
And I'll also bet my acreage that someday
I will be seeing them in court as well.

On the Sunny Side of the Ocean

We always met at a small, round table
sipping our chamomile in a tea room
on a wharf loaded with beer joints,
wine bars, and whatever other
as we called them
"drunken holes" there were.

For months, I held it inside,
but as the lowering sun shone through
the storefront window into my eyes
and she told me in passing about her thirty-year-old daughter
finally kicking that habit, I let out that long, deep breath
and told her the circumstances of my wife of thirty years' death.

And in such a way that I never before could fathom,
the lips across from me quivered with a sensuous lure,
the cheeks flushed with an angelic ambiance,
the auburn hair glowed delicately from the casting rays,
and I swear I had discovered a gravitational pull of peace
on the sunny side of the ocean.

Desert Storm at High Noon

Teddy Roosevelt's grandson stepped
off his camel.

"If Jimmy Carter had balls, he would have
stepped down from the helicopter
and blown those Iranians to Timbuktu."

The Supreme Court justice stepped off his horse.

"No, if Jimmy Carter had balls, he would have
stepped up and apologized to the Iranian people
for Operation Ajax and the way
Savak broke their backs."

Café Bohemia

If only I had been born earlier.

For I couldn't ask for anything more
than to be there on the corner
of Barrow and West Fourth,
looking out at the triangular
Sheridan Square in the twilight
while waiting in line to see
the Miles Davis Quintet.

That's right, George and Ira,
who could ask for anything more.

I wondered what they were going to play,
a Gershwin tune, maybe.

I wasn't the only one wondering:
Ginsberg and Kerouac scratched
their heads over which way
Whitman's beard pointed.

Kerouac talked about
how Bird looked like Buddha.
Ginsberg began wishing
he were entering a neon fruit supermarket.

We then strolled below the blue
and green haze. I couldn't see above
the third story of the building.

Red fluorescence poured through
the arched window atop the doors
as if we were passing under a setting sun.

Whitman's beard pointed at the table
front and center, and that's where we sat.

Booze flowed in and out of iced glasses,
but because I hadn't been born yet,
I was too young to drink it.

But the coffee was hot and blue
just like a Bean solo.

Miles appeared under the red light.
Eddie Jefferson was right:
The fit of his clothes perfect.

Miles shook hands with Red, as
a conductor does with his concertmaster.

He blew his horn at Philly Joe's nodding head
and wiped strands of spaghetti and hot sauce
from Paul's chin.

Tingling sensations poured out from Red's keys,
carrying the rhythm before Philly Joe's sock symbols
picked it up, and Paul's thumping moans pumped it further.

Miles punched a snoring Trane in the stomach.
Monk popped up from the table next to me, his bear's
body staring Miles down. Miles stared back.

Trane stood and put the tenor to his mouth, still
as an immortal statue.

Each note he blew got bigger and bigger until
one popped and shattered my cup.

The liquid splashed straight to my heart.

Parker's Mood

I met a woman
and discovered romanticism.

We talked about our lives,
and I discovered realism.

We weren't right for each other,
and I discovered pessimism.

Parker's Mood bopped into my head,
and I discovered the blues.

Spirit of '76

The latest campaign slogan
just came across my dusty desk:
"Make American Great Again."
This leads to the obvious question.

When was America great?
Let's blow some dust off the bookshelves,
turn back the gray pages,
and find out when that time was.

First, we gave the people below us
the freedom of choice:
Work for us or go to prison.

Unfortunately, building more prisons
was not cost effective. So, we decided
to send them to west of the Appalachians.

Unfortunately, the oppressors from above
said no. We fought for our freedom
to do this. And we won.

America became great. All it took was to
slip in the necessary funds
to put the right people in the right places.

Unfortunately, some foreign element
came along and dictated
that we can't do that.

We then slipped in the necessary funds
to a select few, and they gave us our
freedom back. That was just six years ago.

So to say "Make America Great Again"
just doesn't make sense, for this country
has always been great.

Take Five

The distinction between
cultural honor and
my personal honor
ain't all that easy
to make.

Running Red Blood

Out from my smoldering tepee,
I ran the shoulder of the highway
alongside cars rumbling to and from
the chemical plant.

I arrived at a road paved in white.
The houses were white.
The picket fences were white.
That's right; everything was white.

I could be white too if I ran
this road. But as I passed a group
of gentlemen dressed in white,
one yelled, "Do you own a mailbox here?"

I about-faced, and as I passed them again,
I quipped that I could tell that I was
not welcomed here. They didn't even
give me a nod.

I ran back down the road and found myself
running across the smoldering Cuyahoga River.
On the other side, my feet were caked in coals of mud.
But that's okay, because the road was black, too.

And so were the crooked roofs and windows and doors
framed by the planks and sacks and poles.
And so were the clothes of gangs of men
brandishing their pistols and rifles at me.

I raised my chest and fists to the smoldering sky
and screamed from the top of my lungs, "That's right.
I'm a white motherfucker
so go ahead and shoot me."

Windy City Values

Okay, who would like the honors
of going first?
"Me, me, me, me."

Okay, Sammy. Start us off.
"I wanna be a firefighter."
That's wonderful. Now, tell us why.
"Because the town will burn up, otherwise."
That's a perfectly good reason.

Okay, Jessie.
"I wanna be a drug dealer."
Now, Jessie. You know that's illegal.
"Okay, I'll be a pharmacist."
And that will make you very popular.

Okay, Jackie.
"I wanna be a doctor."
That's wonderful. And tell us why.
"Because the money's so good."
Oh, okay. Bobby, what's up?

"I wanna be a cop."
That's equally wonderful. Tell us why.
"For the same reason as Jackie."
But policemen don't make that kind of dough.
"Not so if you know how to do it right."

If You Value Your Life, You Won't Make a Stink

It was a pleasant commute from one end of the island
to the other. Firs, cedars, and broadleaf maples
loomed over the two-lane winding road, where commuters
cruised past stoplights that seemingly rarely turned red.

One late afternoon, on the other side of the bridge,
where the tribal casino was, the light not only didn't
rarely run red, but also stayed red for an additional
twenty seconds, and that doubled the commuter time.

Seemingly faster than the light could turn green, campaign
donations were given, politicians sought out the cameras
and stately announced the wonderful news, and bulldozers
cleared out the trees for a sparkling new four-lane road.

Free Market Enterprise

Sure, you can cut in front of me.
It's a free country.
You can do whatever you want.

And so can I consume the clean air
and puff clouds of smoke
all over your back.

Air Pollution

I am at a rest stop and start
relaxing with a book.

The car is a bit stuffy, so
I roll down the window.

Smoke wafts through the crack.
I look up.

A security guard leans against his BMW
so calm and puffs his cork-tip cigarette

that I snarl, turn the key, rev the engine,
crank the air conditioner, and roll up the window.

The Fine Art of Fundraising

My teacher's contract requires me to be here.
It implies that I be a table captain.
So, I pour another round of drinks.

I know nothing of these seven in the circle
around me, save they have more money
than they know what to do with.

The fundraising chairman schmoozes,
swaggers from table to table, perfectly placed
bronze hair, freckles that shine with every smile …

Save the urgent glance at me about
egging on my table.
So, I pour another round of drinks.

I tell them the two beauties of alcohol:
It lowers their inhibitions, and they're
no longer thinking straight.

Before they can ponder this,
I raise my glass of ginger ale
and give them the concrete sell:

"The money pays for a full-time staff."
Fear of waiting on tables
on nights and weekends creeps into me.

One donor slurs out,
"Last year, it was scholarships
for those in need. Did you do it?"

Before I say no, my prized speech
student takes on the voice of God
at the podium.

As instructed, he pours out
the school's importance to him
and the community.

Many wipe away tears as the bidding
for thousands of dollars of procurements
begins and escalates.

The only problem is no one at
my table has a winning bid.
So, I pour another round of drinks.

My table soon racks up one impetuous win
after another, notably raising the paddle.
My job for next year is guaranteed.

Relief and a salesman's high mix into me
as I push in the clutch and drive my clanking
Beetle into the neon night.

Soothing violins and woodwinds float
through my soul until the DJ pipes in turn
for donations to keep this station on the air.

I turn the dial to the news. The symphony's
highly acclaimed conductor resigns.
The "business end" has been too much.

I find myself strolling to the mall.
Raindrops sting my eyes.
A pickup truck pulls up beside me.

The driver doesn't have enough gas to get
home. Yet, he has tools in his flatbed
he's willing to sell for next to nothing.

As I turn away, a lady looking
like the grandmother of my prized
speech student sobs to me her story:

She came from far away to visit her son. He's
nowhere to be found after his landlord evicted
him. She's out of money for a place to stay.

On my way back to the Beetle, a young man
with a boy at his side asks me for spare
change, so he and his son can have dinner.

After my apologetic lie, a free-flowing
golden grayed hair man approaches on a
mountain bike I used to own before my Beetle.

He asks for a few bucks.
I toss him my bulging wallet.
He catches it on the fly and rides off with the wind.

One Man, One Vote

Let me make one thing
perfectly clear:

Yes, it's a sad state
of affairs when an attorney
general has to beg for money
to keep his job.

But for you
I'll do it.

How You Can Sell Anything to Anyone

In November 2016, Hillary Clinton nearly
became the first woman to break
the glass ceiling, but she lost
to the first woman to run
a successful presidential campaign.

How To Get a Gig

We want you to have a presence.

I can pull an Iggy Pop,
rolling around in broken glass,
singing "I got my cock in my pocket."

Well, not that much.

I can pull a Jim Morrison,
yanking down my pants,
exposing my privates and all that.

Better but not that much.

I can swirl my balls,
singing B-I-N-G-O, B-I-N-G-O
B-I-N-G-O and Bingo was his name O
between calling out the letters and numbers.

Bingo.

Not Taught at the Conservatory

The case echoed shut.
The night of mumbles, grumbles,
and lukewarm applauses was over.

A lady waddled to the stage
and frowned.

"You should've played some
rock and roll."

"You can't be serious."

She pointed her cane at him.
"Like Neil Diamond."

"Why."

"I saw him in concert once.
I was so up close
I could see the hairs on his chest."

"I'm sorry ma'am; his compositions,
if he wrote any, haven't made it
into my repertoire."

"No matter.
I was so up close at his concert
I could see the hairs on his chest."

The Fine Art of Filling Prison Cells

The night shined with an Artimus glow.
I drove past two deer resting on the asphalt.
Their antlers glowed in gold. Undoubtedly, tourists
zoomed by earlier and took pictures of them.

As I pulled into my personal parking spot,
a police car sprinted past the deer.
It howled like a pair of hounds
pursuing prey.

It stopped at a dumpster just past our condo
complex: A woman sat, body lowered
as if grazing the grass, and a man lay under
a broken down cardboard box.

They were loaded into the police car,
taken away to where
the sun remained a secret
and the moon smiled.

"Cut the Bullshit, Vote for Trump"

President-elect Donald Trump hoofs
to the podium. The reporters' eyes twitch,
and they pinch their noses.

One raises his hand.
"With all respect sir, why do you look and smell
as if you're covered with layers of horseshit."

President-elect Trump whinnies.
"That's not the problem. The problem is you need
to have your senses checked."

Politically Speaking

One thing you've got to admit.
You sure got a great surname.

Just like Greg Pruitt.
Remember him?

Oklahoma All-American.
Cleveland Browns All-Pro.

Quick on one's feet
as one can be.

Just think.
If only you were like that.

Or as much as your ex-boss is.
You'd still have your job today.

Power Struggle

Big Ben leans over the lectern
and turns the page
to the oldest trick in the book:

"For the elite to stay in power,
it must convince the populace
of an outside threat."

The senators on the floor nod
in acknowledgment.

The representatives behind them nod
in acknowledgment.

The boom-boom suppliers in the stands nod
in acknowledgment.

The reporters jot this down.

That's right.
All of this has been well documented.
But it continues to happen.

Who Won the War, Daddy?

To M.T. Anderson

Well son, I'll tell you all
about the Great Patriotic War.

Before it started, anyone disagreeing
that life was getting better was taken away
at midnight by the Black Maria.

Then again, none of this mattered if his number
fell into the regional arrest quota. Meat and
vegetable trucks then snuck him away.

Many writhed on basement floors from boots
and steel rods to the face, ribs, and belly before
confessing to crimes nobody committed.

The rest were submitted to pre-dawn bursts
of shootings in a fortress
under the shadows of a church.

The NKVD head, twenty thousand secret police, three
of our top five marshals, thirteen army commanders,
and twenty-seven thousand officers and soldiers were all gone.

It didn't take a Napoleon to realize we were ripe
for a takeover. And that's what those
invading brutes in horned helmets set out to do.

As they shot down our antiquated planes and more than half
of what was left of our ill-equipped army, we showered
these liberators with gifts and even fought for them.

But in their hubris, they enslaved, beat, and shot us
to death. So, we took to the woods and came out
hell-bent on ripping them apart with our bare hands.

Their hubris continued, promising a takeover by winter.
But from the summer rains trucks couldn't
get through the muck to supply their tanks.

When the winter storms came, their supply
lines were too long and thin to provide
ammo and heavy coats.

Their planes couldn't rise from the frozen
ground. When our land thawed, their tanks
wouldn't start at all.

Under Order 270, we fought those defenseless
creatures to the death. Any of us caught
being taken prisoner would be shot.

Before we knew it, we marched across
their border to the prison camps, busted through
the barbed-wire fences, and shot our own men.

Operation Ajax

It's all so simple.
Funnel more money to the CIA.
History has shown it works.

Go ahead and bribe
the brothers of Saudi Arabia
and all our other dictators.

It makes our businesses great
and in turn our country great
and in turn our world great.

And if they don't accept our bribes?
Well then, that's where Teddy Roosevelt's
grandson comes into play.

Homage to Kermit Roosevelt

What's your kid gonna do with his degree?

Overthrow governments for the CIA.

Don't you have better bullshit than that?

Can you think of a more patriotic line of work?

Okay, I believe you.

Critical Thinking

He wipes the white foam from his bushy mustache.

"Hey, it's my old James Madison College professor.
Come belly up here next to me.
I'll buy you a beer, and I'll tell you why."

He pats the professor's shoulder, and they drink.

"Remember when you staggered into class,
reeking of bourbon? You rattled
on about the philosophical argument you had
with the dean? You stopped
when I came up to you and told you
your fly was down?"

They clink their labeled Miller Lite
glasses together, sip,
and wipe the foam from their mustaches.

"Oh yes. I know you should be buying me
the drink. But I'm buying the drink
as a means of expressing my gratitude.
You want to know the problem
with kids these days?
They don't know critical thinking!"

He takes two gulps of beer.

"I go into work day-after-day
and see nothing but these perfectly groomed,
blank-faced kids just going through the motions
of punching at their keyboards. They might
as well be AI robots. But you, almighty
professor, you taught us critical thinking."

He finishes his beer, foam hanging
on the rim of the glass
and his mustache.

"That's right, you taught us the logical
progression of how learning to think
critically leads to thinking outside the box,
which liberates us to free and fresh ideas,
such as when we passed all those
legalization of marijuana laws."

He licks the foam off the rim
of the glass and slams it down.
White spent bubbles sink to the bottom.

"Now as I was saying.
What was I saying.
Oh yeah.
Bartender, another beer please."

Drugs

It never ceases to amaze me
how long people are willing
to wait in line
for a cup of coffee.

The Good Earth

Tucked away in a cozy corner of the world
is a small town called Chimacum. It began
and got by on acres of cow pastures. But like
anything else on the good earth, it changed.

Named after a Virginian aristocrat, the county
continues to carry the distinction of being
recognized by the Feds as an economically
distressed area, but that does not account for
the recent arrival of the green elite.

Their patriarch is called "King" because that's
the county, past two bodies of water eastward,
where he amassed his high-tech fortune.
And now it's time to put some of those funds
to good personal use—loading up on the most
wholesome food that money can buy.

He moseys along the cozy aisles
of the corner natural grocery store,
mingling with others from his coterie.
Finally, he passes the cashier, dropping off
a wad of bills for his gallon of raw milk
and packages of raw cheese, thanks
to the raw dairy farm three peninsulas westward.

He dumps his provisions into his
cigarette lighter powered cooler,
takes a left out of the lot, and moseys down
the highway a bit past Center Road. To his left,
he has a choice of two marijuana joints.
He pulls into the one adjacent to the café
featuring local organic farm food.

He places a wad of bills on the counter for
a couple of perfectly rolled, pencil thin joints,
and of course a couple of brownies.
He joins his coterie in the circle.
He lights up, puffs, and passes a joint to his neighbor.
The joint moves from neighbor to neighbor.

Amidst tokes, coughs, county complaints,
and glances at the cemetery across the highway,
their bodies advance with age—eyebrows whiten,
cheeks wrinkle, chins sag. When the cemetery begins
to fade to black, their shaking hands shake goodbye.

Hunched over the wheel, he turns onto the highway
and drives or more like weaves toward Center Road.
His head sweats, wobbles, spins until it spatters
to the floor mat. Shards of bones follow.

Fire trucks from the other side of the highway
and Center Road hurry over and put out the flames.
They roll him into the cemetery and dump him into a pit.

Dvorak's New World Symphony in the New Millennium

A modern NFL stadium personifies the oligarchy.

Olympic National Park says the government shutdown
from Santa Claus means no ski revenue.
Very little snow is on Hurricane Ridge.

A first scrutiny of Walgreen's aisles reveals rows of packaged
food and drink labeled with runaway lists of chemical products.
Beyond the other aisles of jars and cartons of approved experiments
stand, behind a counter, white attired saviors for every ailment.

One-third of Trader Joe's is filled with wine and sugar.

A Doberman pinscher sprints from a lady babbling on her iPhone
and bites a baby in a stroller.
The lady takes a bullet to the brain, and the wounds
spread like a cancer that no one can fix.

Corona Avenue

Below the neon green and white
"Spartan Grocery," a handwritten
sign in Marlboro red reads,
"Facemasks are mandatory.
No if's, and's, or but's."

Below the sign, the clerk
sits on a curbstone, her belly
stretching the contours of her
green and white checkered apron.
Her mask hangs below her chin.

She takes a long drag from
her cigarette, puffs smoke
into the passing exhaust fumes.
She yells above the traffic
into her iPhone.

"Did you read that?
Fat people
are more prone to die
from the virus. What sick shit
will they come up with next?"

She jumps up.
She points at her fanny
and wiggles it at the traffic.
"Well, those people
can kiss my big, fat ass."

She stomps her cigarette
into the crack in the sidewalk
and steps forward.
She puts on her mask.
The front door slides open for her.

Picked from the Apple Tree

You know you
mastered
this millennium

when you can
type
with your thumbs.

Avoid Ambiguous Pronouns

The ladies of the League
of Women Voters sit
around the big, round table.

"I just received a text
from my Julliard grad
son," one says.

"He just received
a text
from Jay Inslee."

"Wow," another says.
"You mean the we're
all in this together Jay Inslee?"

She sips her tea
between her
face mask and lips.

She lowers the empty cup
to the bleach-whitened tablecloth
and wipes it with a sanitizer.

"Wow," another says.
"You mean the no live
music Jay Inslee?"

She refills the cup
and wipes the porcelain
pitcher with a sanitized cloth.

"Yep and Yep. It says he is offering
him six hundred a week to play
his piano in his bedroom."

Cedars in the New Millennium

My favorite pastime
is deleting e-mails

from the screen.
Like swatting flies.

Portrait of a Contemporary Hermit

Whenever I turn off
my cell phone,
I find myself saying,
"Now I can relax."